Monoline Calligraphy Workbook For Beginners

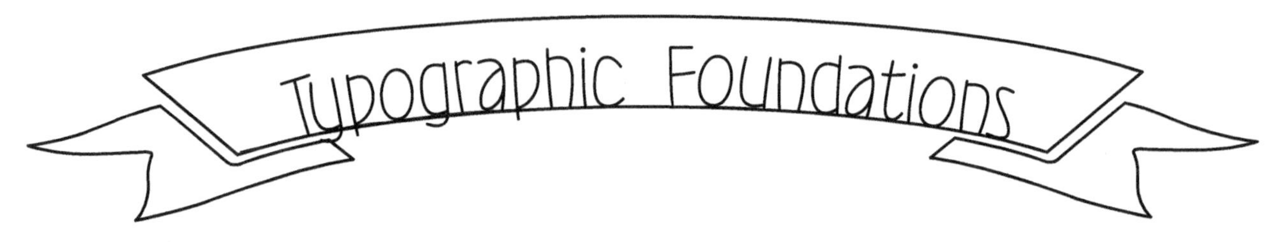

Let's keep it simple—monoline calligraphy isn't about strict rules or complex techniques. It's about consistency, precision, and letting your natural style shine through. The secret? Good posture, a steady grip, and quality paper. These foundations ensure smooth, even strokes and help you create effortlessly balanced designs. Once you master these basics, your pen will glide across the page with confidence and grace.

Body

Think posture doesn't matter? Think again! In monoline calligraphy, precision and control are key. Sit comfortably—preferably at a desk where your feet rest flat on the ground and your arm has room to move smoothly. The secret to even, consistent strokes lies in engaging your entire arm, not just your fingers. Picture yourself composing each line like a steady rhythm—intentional, balanced, and effortlessly fluid.

Pen

Your pen is your tool of precision, and in monoline calligraphy, simplicity is key. Whether it's a fineliner or gel pen, the best tool is one that feels natural in your hand. Hold it upright with a steady, comfortable grip. Don't worry about perfection—your first lines might be uneven, but that's part of the learning process. Monoline calligraphy is about consistency, practice, and letting your style develop with every stroke

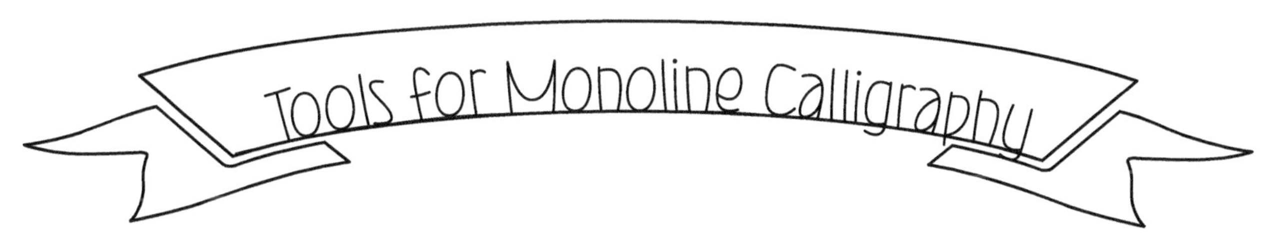

Monoline calligraphy is a celebration of simplicity, precision, and balance. Unlike other calligraphy styles, it focuses on consistent, even strokes, allowing you to create clean and elegant designs without the need for varied pressure. To achieve this, you don't need an extensive collection of supplies—just a few reliable tools will set you on the right path. Here's a more detailed breakdown of what you'll need:

★ Pencils

A pencil is your starting point for every project. Whether you're sketching letterforms or planning a composition, pencils offer the flexibility to experiment and erase mistakes. Go for an HB or slightly harder lead for precise lines without smudging. A mechanical pencil can also be a great option for consistent line width.

★ Fine-Tip Pens

The heart of monoline calligraphy lies in your choice of pen. Fine-tip pens, such as gel pens, technical pens, or fineliners, deliver the smooth and consistent linework that defines this style. Look for pen sizes ranging from 0.3 mm to 0.7 mm for intricate details or slightly bolder strokes. Brands like Micron, Uni-ball, or Staedtler are excellent choices for quality and consistency.

★ Markers

For larger-scale projects or bolder monoline lettering, markers are a fantastic option. Choose markers with fine or medium-sized tips to maintain the uniformity of your strokes. Alcohol-based markers, like those from Sharpie or Copic, work beautifully on smooth surfaces.

★ High-Quality Paper

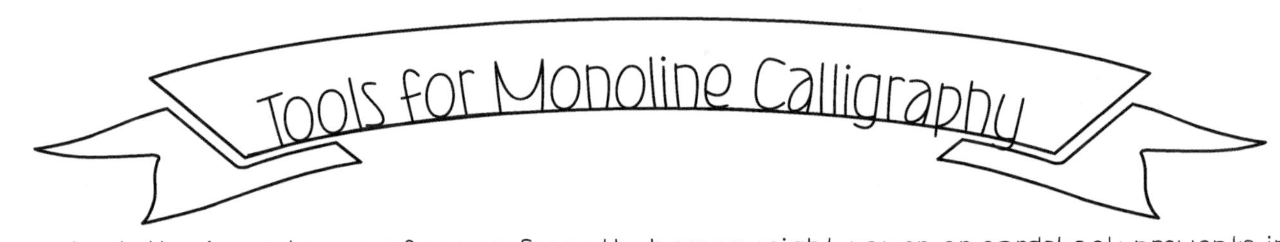

Don't overlook the importance of paper. Smooth, heavyweight paper or cardstock prevents ink from bleeding or feathering, ensuring your work looks polished. Paper designed for calligraphy or illustration, such as bristol board or marker paper, provides an ideal surface for crisp, clean lines.

★ Erasers

A soft eraser is essential for perfecting your pencil sketches before adding ink. Look for a kneaded eraser for delicate adjustments or a plastic eraser for removing larger areas cleanly without tearing the paper.

★ Ruler

A ruler is invaluable for creating guidelines and maintaining consistent letter height, width, and alignment. Straight, clean lines provide structure to your lettering and help ensure a balanced composition.

★ Optional: Compass or Circle Templates

For circular or curved designs, a compass or circle stencil can help you achieve perfect symmetry and proportions, especially in more intricate compositions.

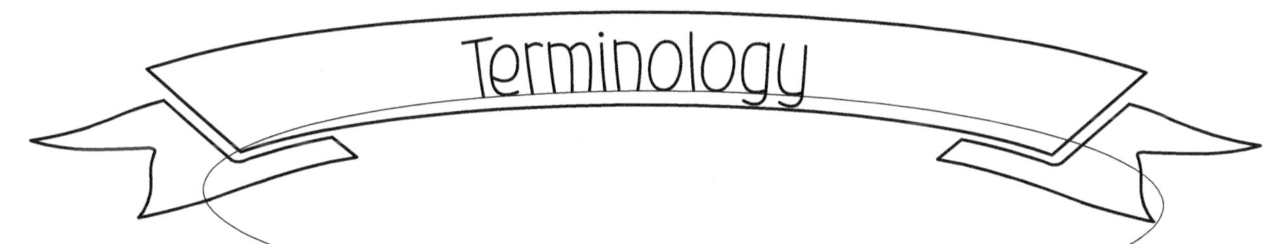

Before you can start crafting clean and elegant letters, it's important to familiarize yourself with a few key terms. Think of this step as learning the building blocks of your craft—like mastering the alphabet before forming words. Don't skip it! A solid understanding of these basics will make your monoline calligraphy journey smoother, more enjoyable, and far more rewarding.

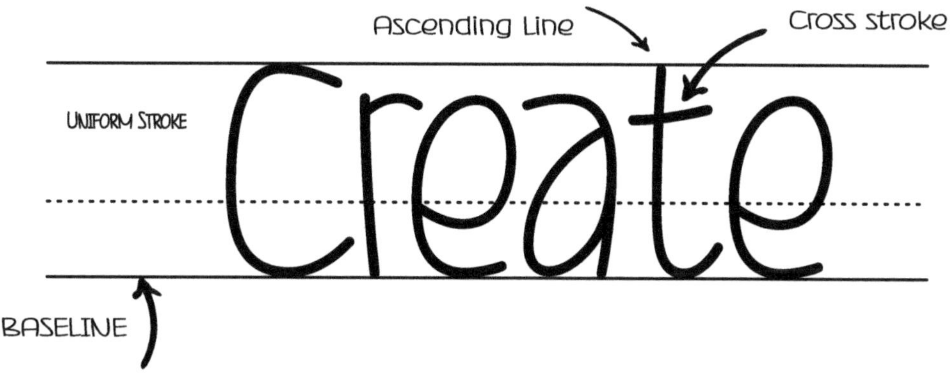

Ascending Line

Marks the upper boundary for letters with ascenders, such as "t" or "l." This line ensures consistent letter height and helps maintain balanced proportions throughout your composition.

Uniform Stroke

A fundamental feature of monoline calligraphy. All lines—both upward and downward strokes—have the same consistent thickness, creating a clean and orderly appearance that defines the style.

Cross Stroke

The horizontal line found in letters like "t." This structural element adds character and reinforces the shape of the letters, contributing to their overall harmony.

Baseline

The foundational line on which all letters rest. It provides stability and alignment, ensuring a cohesive and visually appealing word structure.

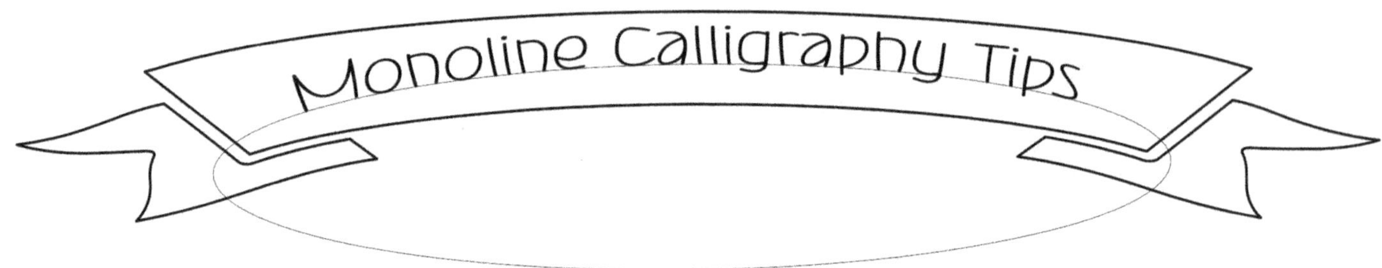

ONE

Slow and steady wins the race! Approach each letter as a small work of art, focusing on precise, even strokes instead of rushing like with ordinary handwriting.

TWO

Start with a pencil—it's your best tool for planning. Sketch, erase, and refine your designs until they look just right. Mistakes? They're all part of the journey!

THREE

Lift your pen after every stroke. Monoline calligraphy relies on deliberate, controlled movements, allowing you to focus on clean and consistent lines for each segment.

FOUR

Forget about varying stroke thickness—monoline is all about consistency. Every stroke, whether upward or downward, maintains the same weight for a polished, balanced appearance.

FIVE

Focus on smooth, steady motions. Let your hand glide evenly to keep your lines clean and uniform, no matter the direction of your stroke.

SIX

Practice makes perfect! Master the shapes of individual letters, then work on connecting them into words. Once you've nailed the basics, experiment with compositions to add your personal flair.

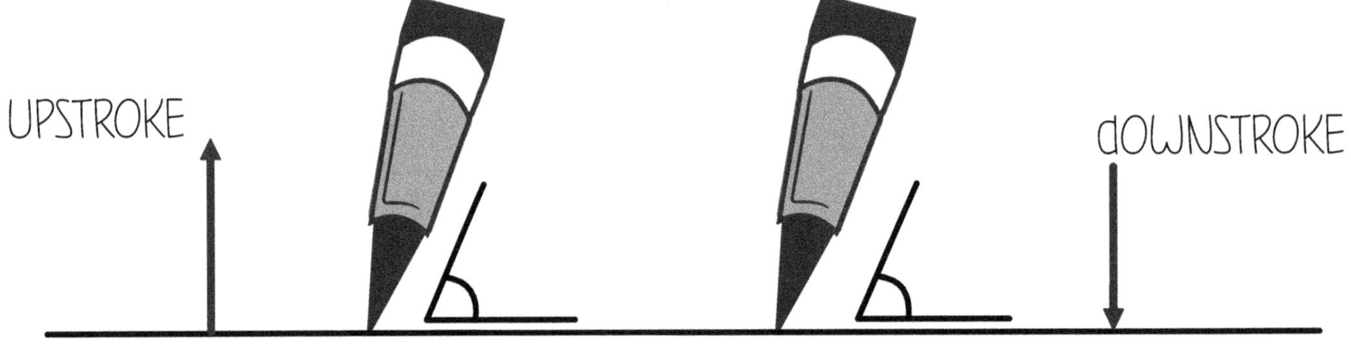

IN THE NEXT SECTION, WE'LL EXPLORE THE ESSENTIALS—MASTERING FOUNDATIONAL STROKES AND CRAFTING BEAUTIFUL LETTERFORMS!PICK UP YOUR PENCIL, FINELINER, OR MARKER—IT'S TIME TO TRANSFORM SIMPLE STROKES INTO ART. YOUR MONOLINE CALLIGRAPHY JOURNEY BEGINS NOW!

Basic strokes
Introduction

ALSO KNOWN AS "FAUX CALLIGRAPHY," THESE STROKES ARE A GREAT STARTING POINT FOR MONOLINE CALLIGRAPHY. WHILE BOLD AND THICK STROKES MAY WORK FOR OTHER STYLES, MONOLINE FOCUSES ON CONSISTENCY, MAKING IT QUICKER, SIMPLER, AND EFFORTLESSLY ELEGANT.

THIS TECHNIQUE MIRRORS THE FLOW OF BRUSH LETTERING BUT WITHOUT ANY VARIATION IN PRESSURE—EVERY STROKE IS PERFECTLY UNIFORM. WITH JUST A PENCIL OR A FINE-TIP PEN (THE SMALLER, THE BETTER), YOU CAN CREATE CLEAN AND BALANCED DESIGNS. MONOLINE IS ALL ABOUT PRECISION, SO GET READY TO DRAW SMOOTH, CONSISTENT STROKES WITH EASE!

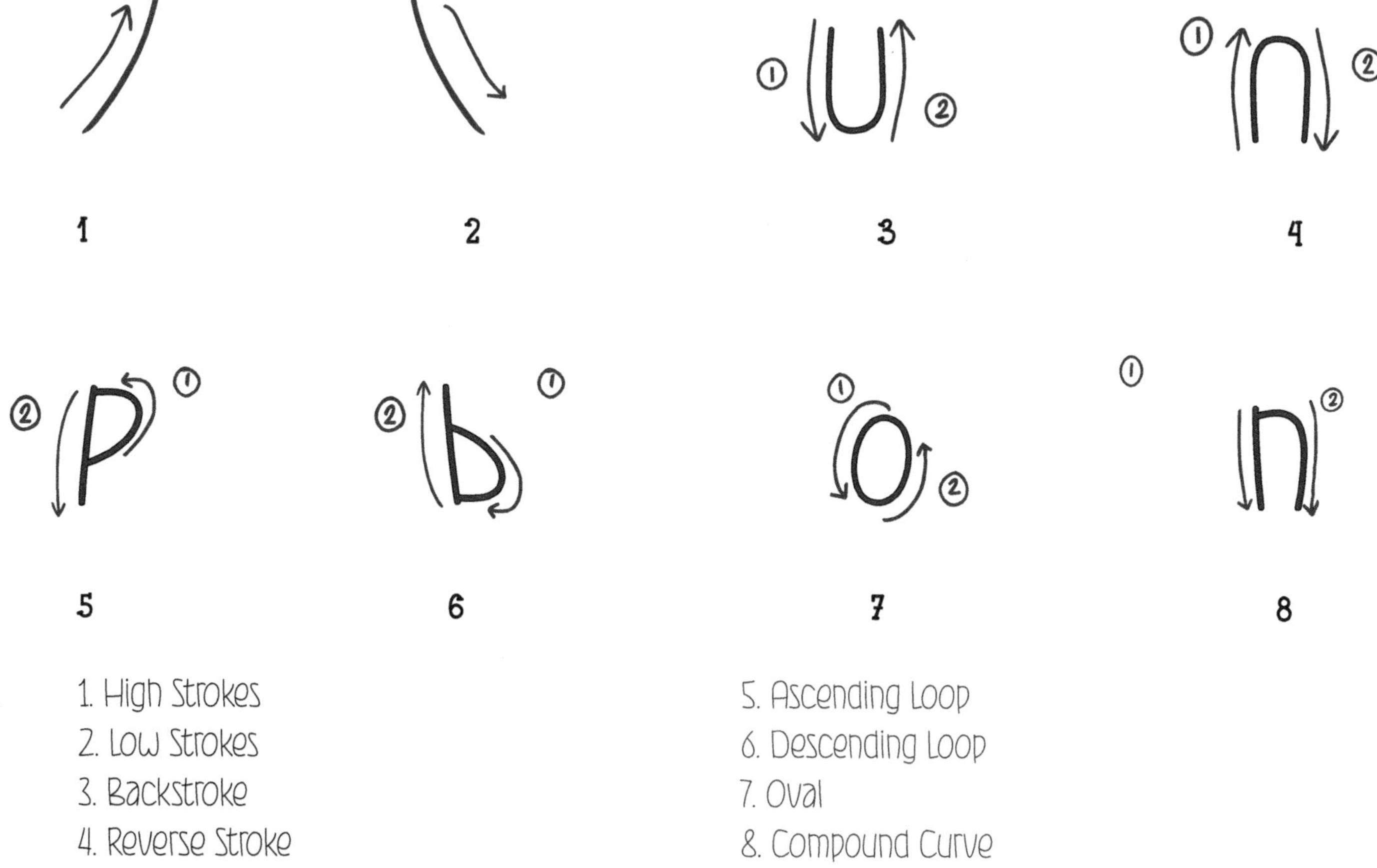

1. High Strokes
2. Low Strokes
3. Backstroke
4. Reverse Stroke
5. Ascending Loop
6. Descending Loop
7. Oval
8. Compound Curve

Upward Strokes

- BEGIN FROM THE BOTTOM, MOVING UPWARD WITH A STEADY AND SMOOTH MOTION.

- MAINTAIN CONSISTENT LINE THICKNESS FOR A CLEAN AND POLISHED APPEARANCE.

- USE A LIGHT, CONTROLLED HAND TO ENSURE AN EVEN, GRACEFUL FLOW THROUGHOUT THE STROKE.

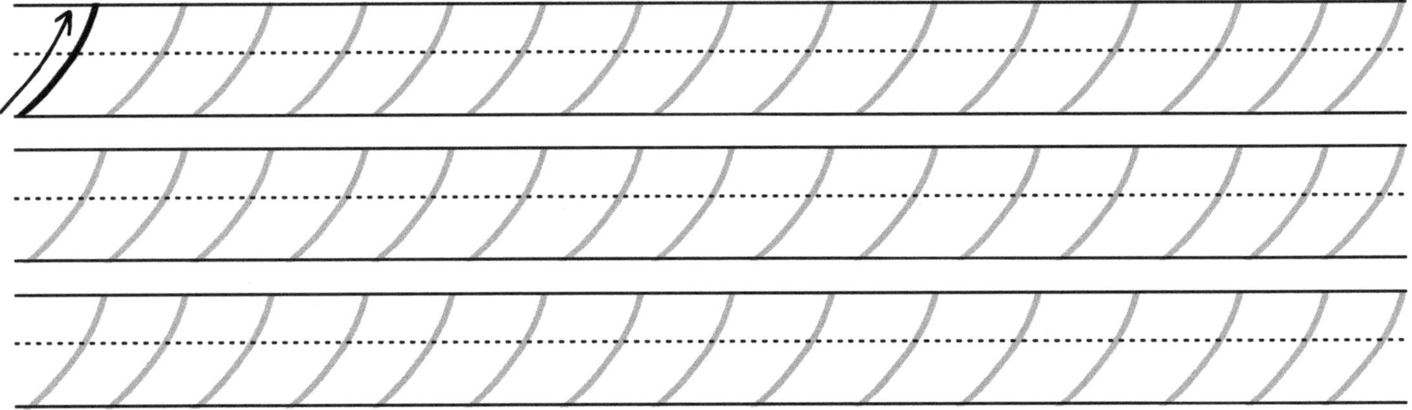

Downward Strokes

- BEGIN AT THE TOP, MOVING DOWNWARD IN A STEADY, CONTROLLED MOTION.

- UNLIKE OTHER STYLES, MAINTAIN CONSISTENT LINE THICKNESS THROUGHOUT THE STROKE—NO PRESSURE VARIATION NEEDED.

- FOCUS ON SMOOTH, EVEN MOVEMENTS FOR A CLEAN AND BALANCED FINISH.

Upturn

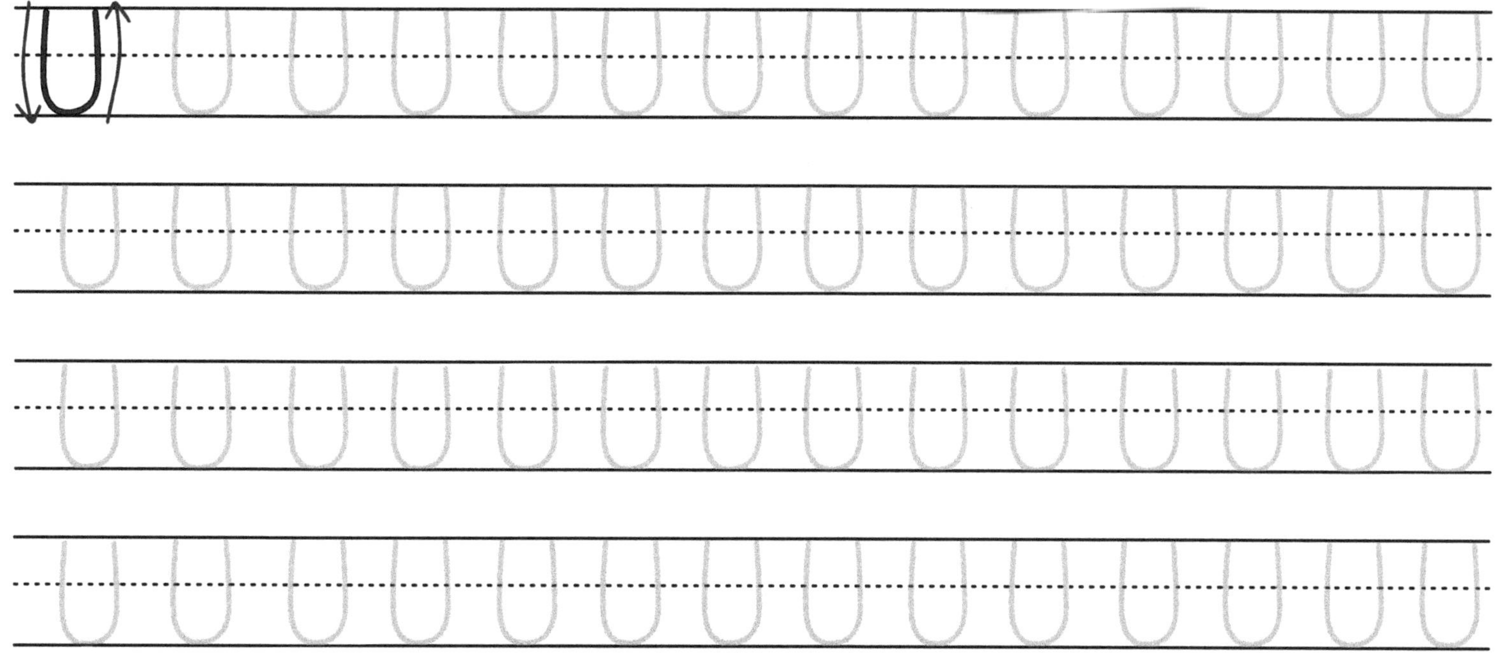

Turnaround

- BEGIN WITH AN UPWARD STROKE, APPLYING LIGHT, CONSISTENT PRESSURE TO CREATE A THIN LINE.

- SMOOTHLY TRANSITION INTO A DOWNWARD STROKE BY INCREASING PRESSURE AS YOU MOVE DOWNWARD.

- THE KEY IS A SEAMLESS FLOW—PRACTICE BLENDING THE THIN UPWARD LINE INTO THE THICKER DOWNWARD STROKE FOR A POLISHED LOOK.

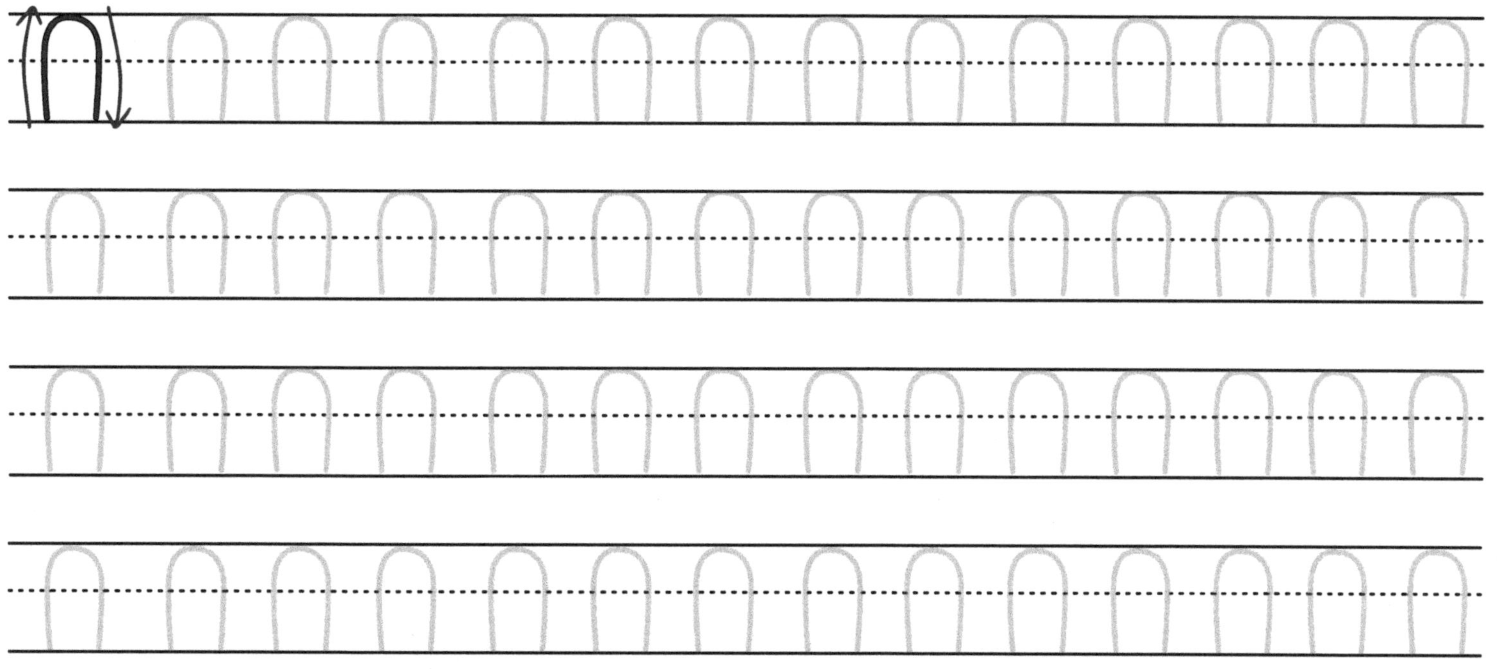

Ascending Loop

Descending Loop

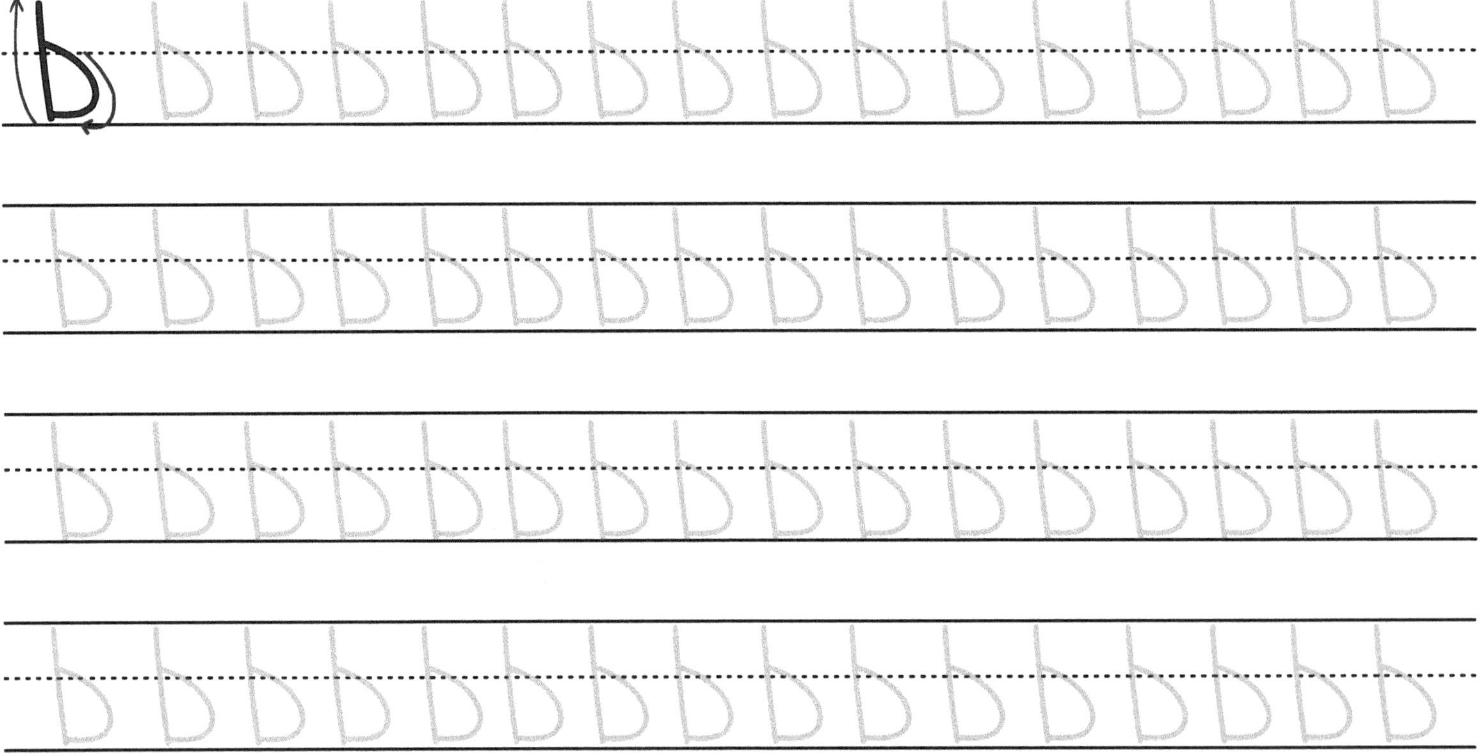

Oval

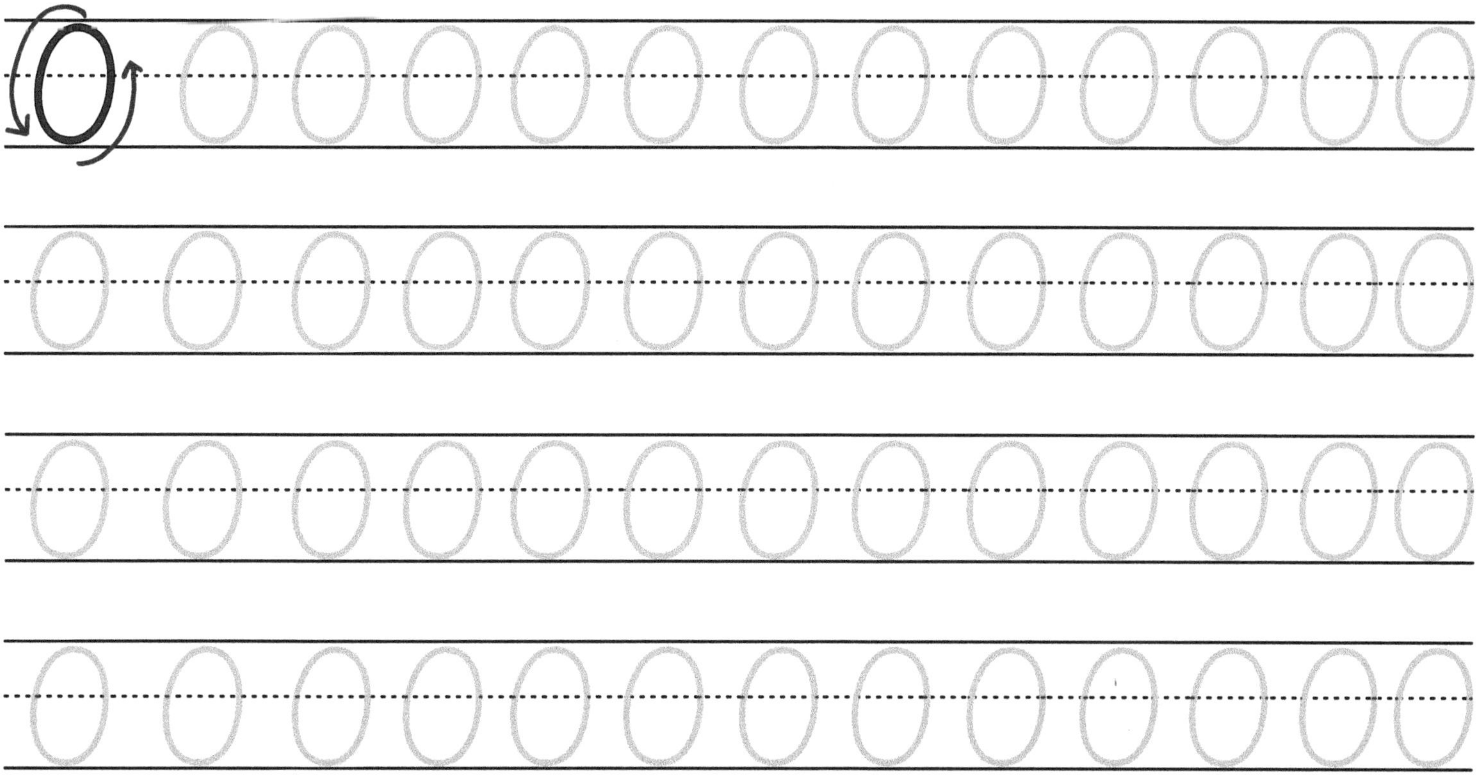

Compression of Turns

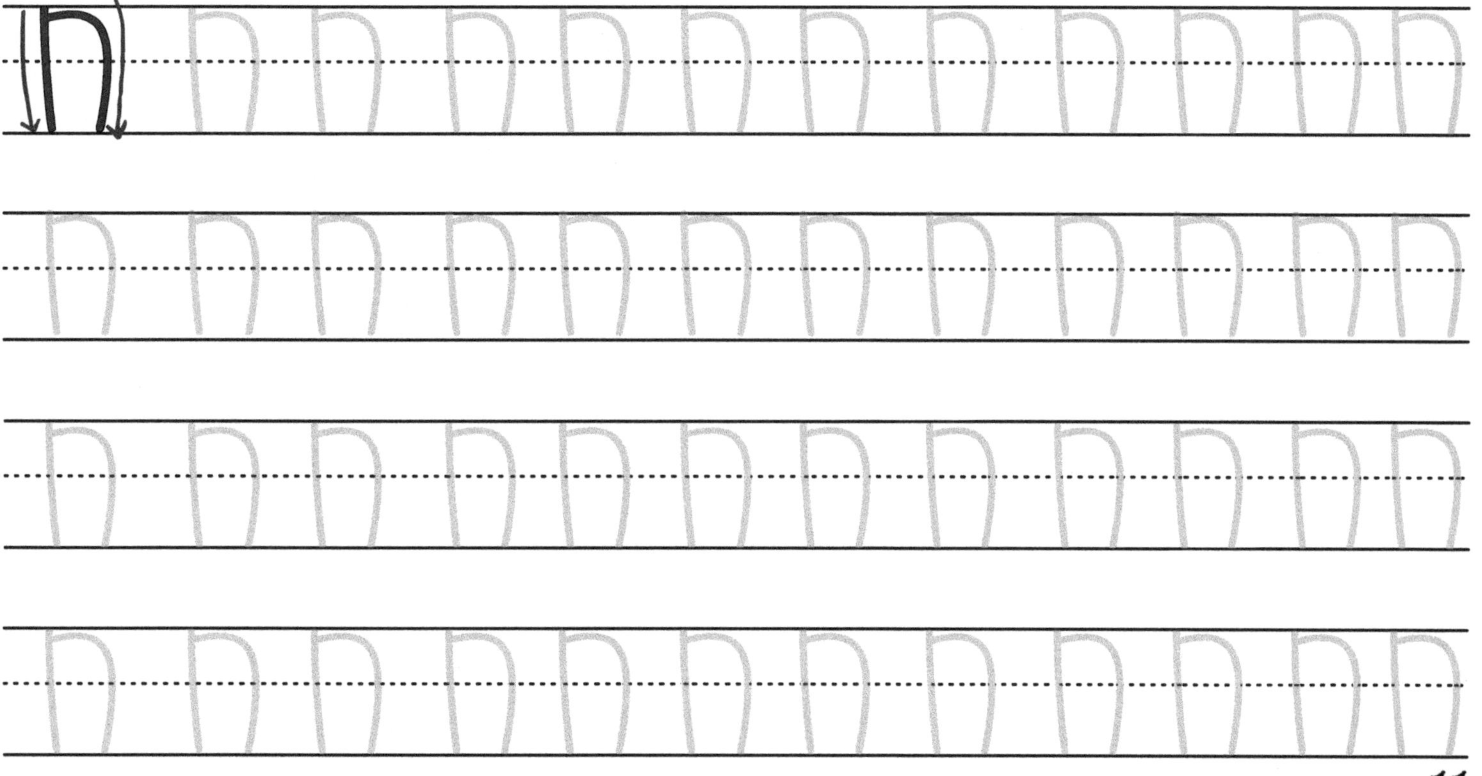

Basic Calligraphy

UPPERCASE ALPHABET - CHARACTER ONE

A A A A A A A A A A A A A A A

B B B B B B B B B B B B B B B

C C C C C C C C C C C C C C C

D D D D D D D D D D D D D D D

E E E E E E E E E E E E E E E

F F F F F F F F F F F F F F F

G G G G G G G G G G G G G G

Practice Sheet

Basic Calligraphy

H H H H H H H H H H H H H H H H H H H

I I I I I I I I I I I I I I I I I I I I I

J J J J J J J J J J J J J J J J J J

K K K K K K K K K K K K K

L L L L L L L L L L L L L L L L L L L L

M M M M M M M M M M M M

N N N N N N N N N N N N

Practice Sheet

Basic Calligraphy

O O O O O O O O O

P P P P P P P P P

Q Q Q Q Q Q Q Q

R R R R R R R R R R

S S S S S S S S S S

T T T T T T T T T T T T

U U U U U U U U U U U

Practice Sheet

Basic Calligraphy

Practice Sheet

Basic Calligraphy

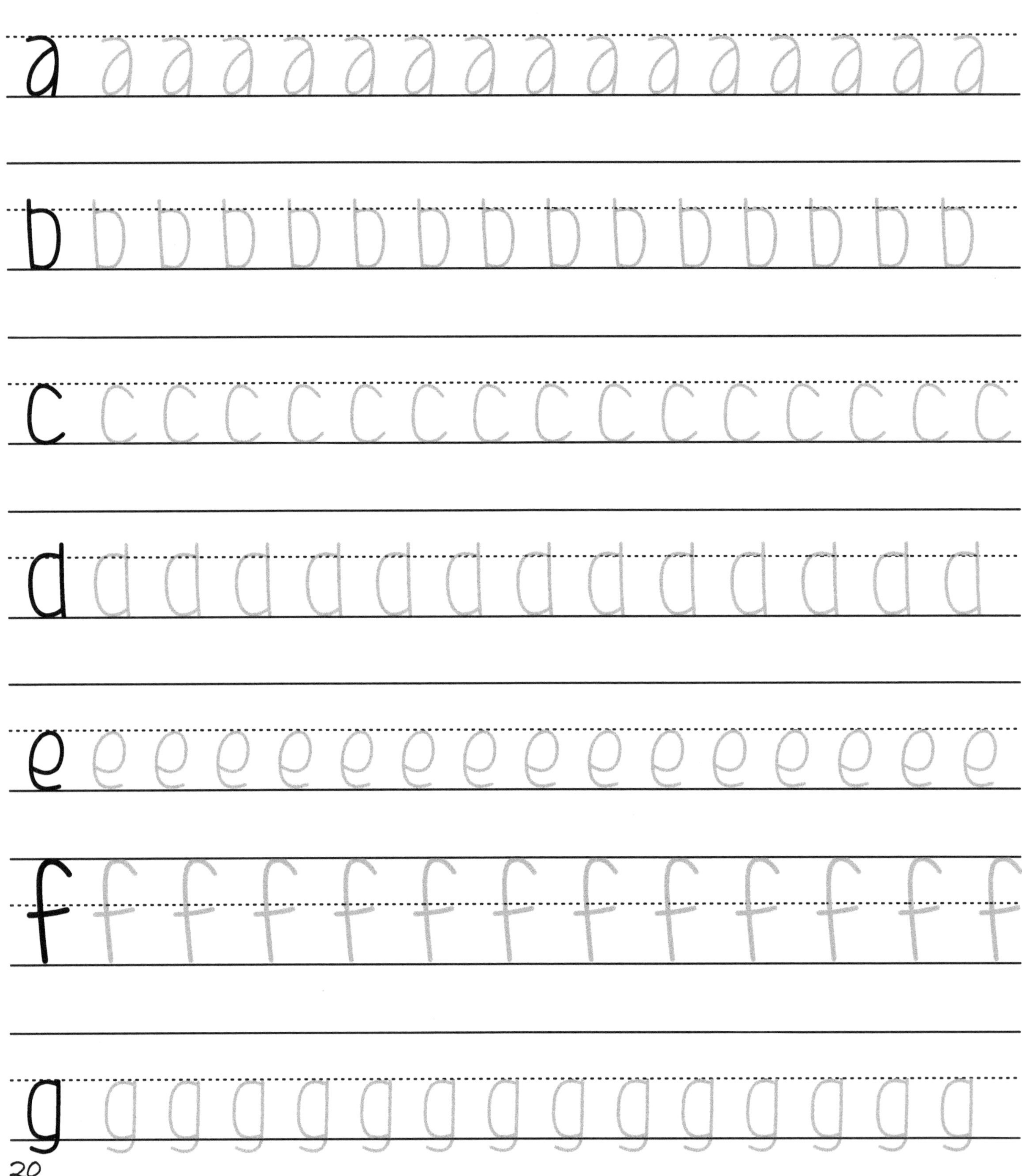

Practice Sheet

Basic Calligraphy

LOWERCASE ALPHABET - CHARACTER ONE

h

i

j

k

l

m

n

Practice Sheet

Basic Calligraphy

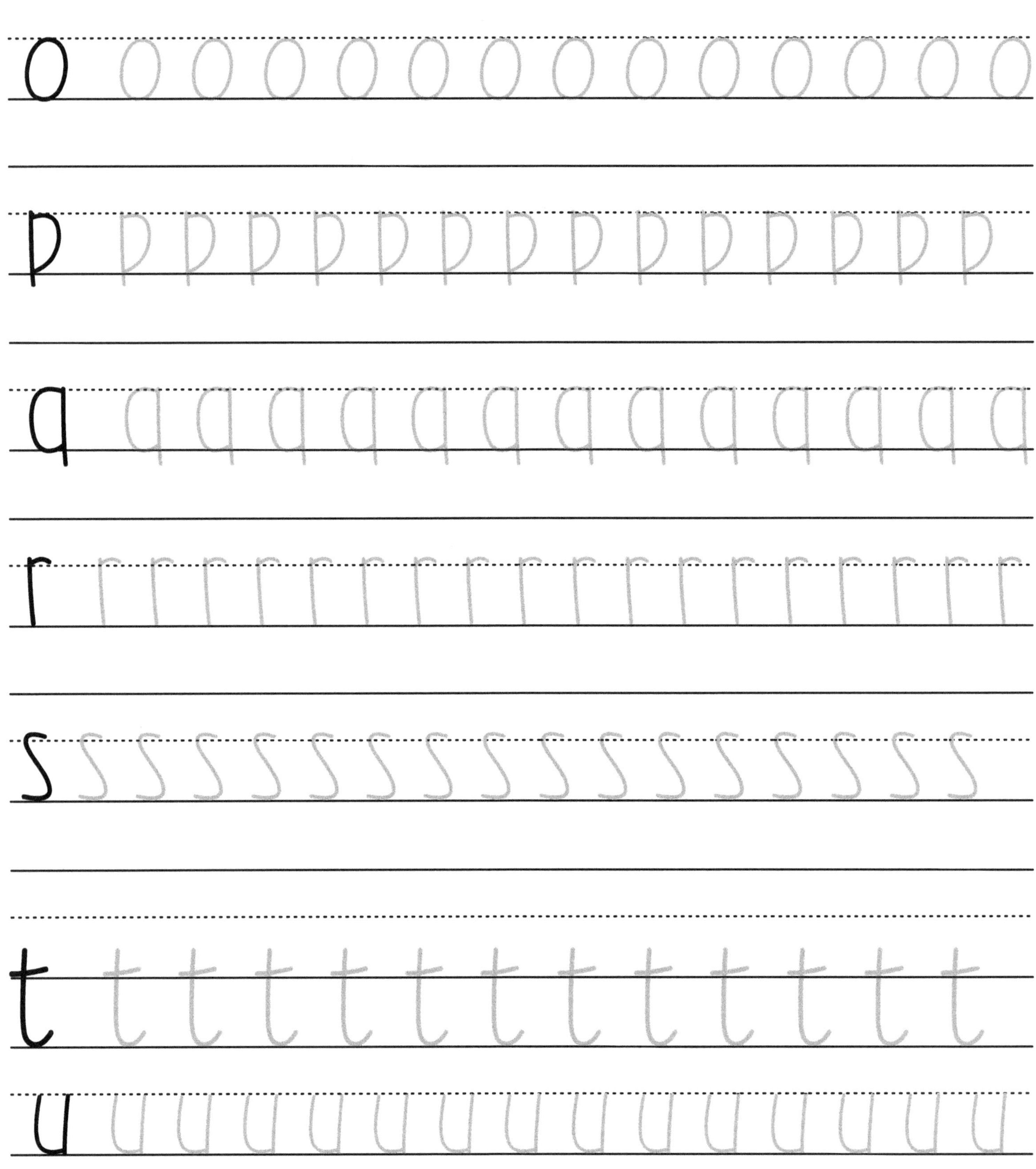

Practice Sheet

Basic Calligraphy

v

w

x

y

z

Practice Sheet

Basic Calligraphy

A A A A A A A A A A

a a a a a a a a a a a a a a a a a a a

B B B B B B B B B B

b b b b b b b b b b b b b b b b b b

C C C C C C C C C C C

c c c c c c c c c c c c c c c c c c c

D D D D D D D D D D D

Practice Sheet

Basic Calligraphy

UPPERCASE AND LOWERCASE PRACTICE

d d d d d d d d d d d d d d d d d d d

E E E E E E E E E E E E E E

e e e e e e e e e e e e e e e e e e e

F F F F F F F F F F F F F F F

f f f f f f f f f f f f f f f f f f

G G G G G G G G G G

g g g g g g g g g g g g g g g g g g

Practice Sheet

Basic Calligraphy

H

b

I

i

J

j

K

Practice Sheet

Basic Calligraphy

Practice Sheet

Basic Calligraphy

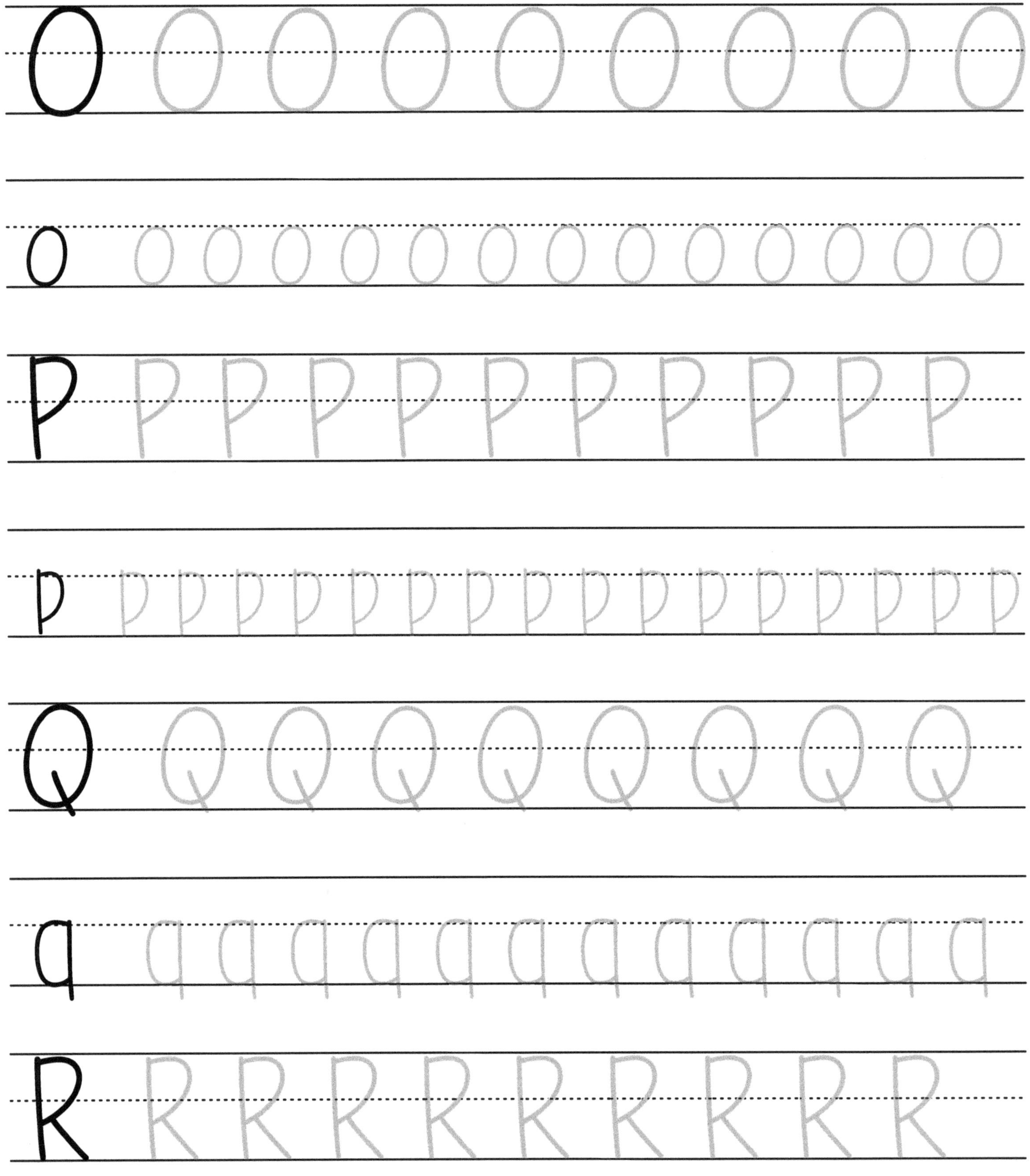

Practice Sheet

Basic Calligraphy

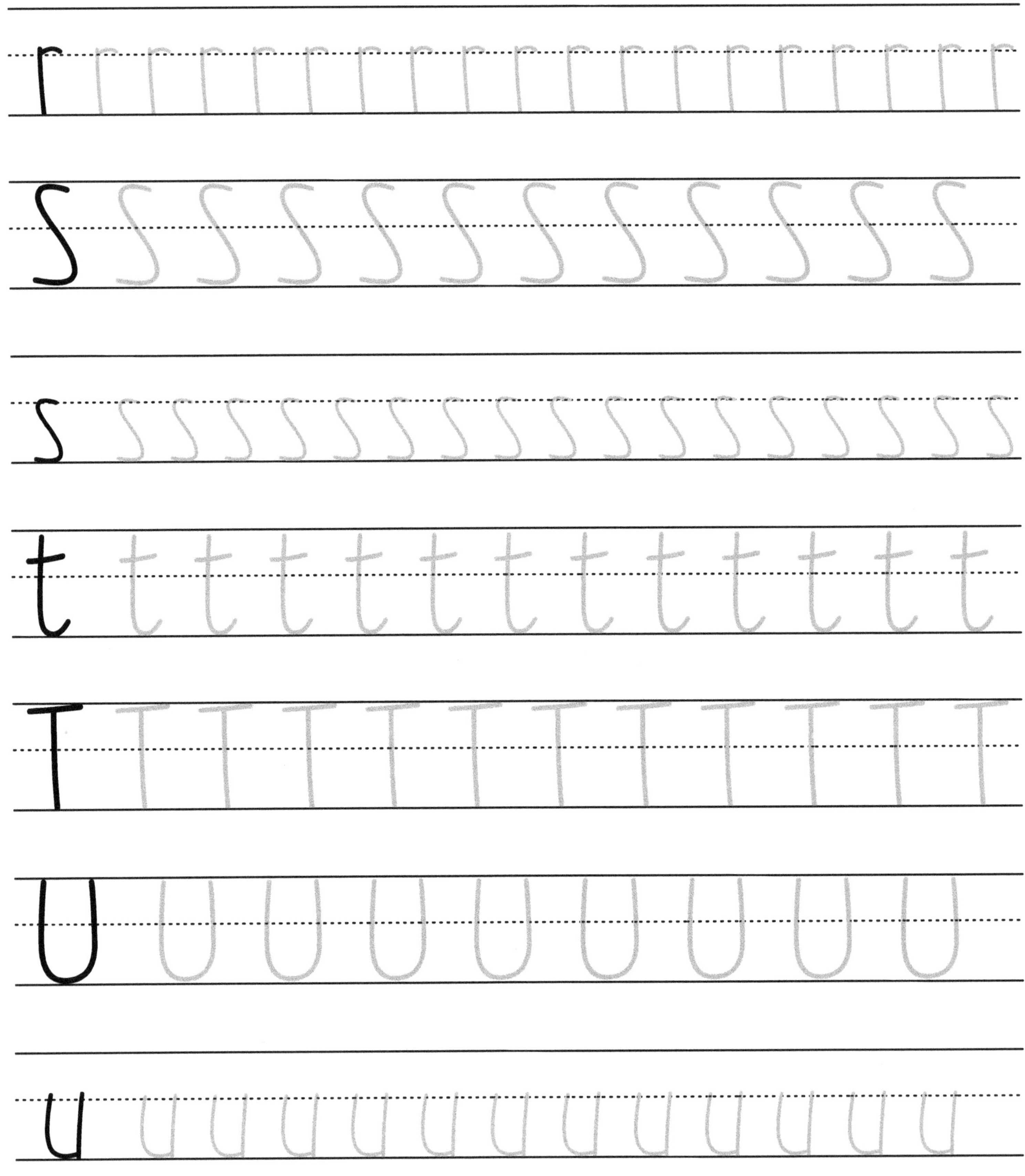

Practice Sheet

Basic Calligraphy

UPPERCASE AND LOWERCASE PRACTICE

Practice Sheet

Basic Calligraphy

y y y y y y y y y y y y y y y y y y y

Z Z Z Z Z Z Z Z Z Z Z

z z z z z z z z z z z z z z z z

Practice Sheet

Basic Calligraphy

0 0 0 0 0 0 0 0 0 0 0

1 1 1 1 1 1 1 1 1 1 1 1 1 1 1 1 1

2 2 2 2 2 2 2 2 2 2 2

3 3 3 3 3 3 3 3 3 3 3

4 4 4 4 4 4 4 4 4 4 4 4

5 5 5 5 5 5 5 5 5 5 5

6 6 6 6 6 6 6 6 6 6 6

Practice Sheet

Basic Calligraphy

7
8
9
10
22
33
44

Practice Sheet

Basic Calligraphy

A A A A A A A A

B B B B B B B B

C C C C C C C C

D D D D D D D D

E E E E E E E E E

F F F F F F F

G G G G G G G G

Practice Sheet

Basic Calligraphy

UPPERCASE ALPHABET - SECOND CHARACTER

Practice Sheet

Basic Calligraphy

UPPERCASE ALPHABET - SECOND CHARACTER

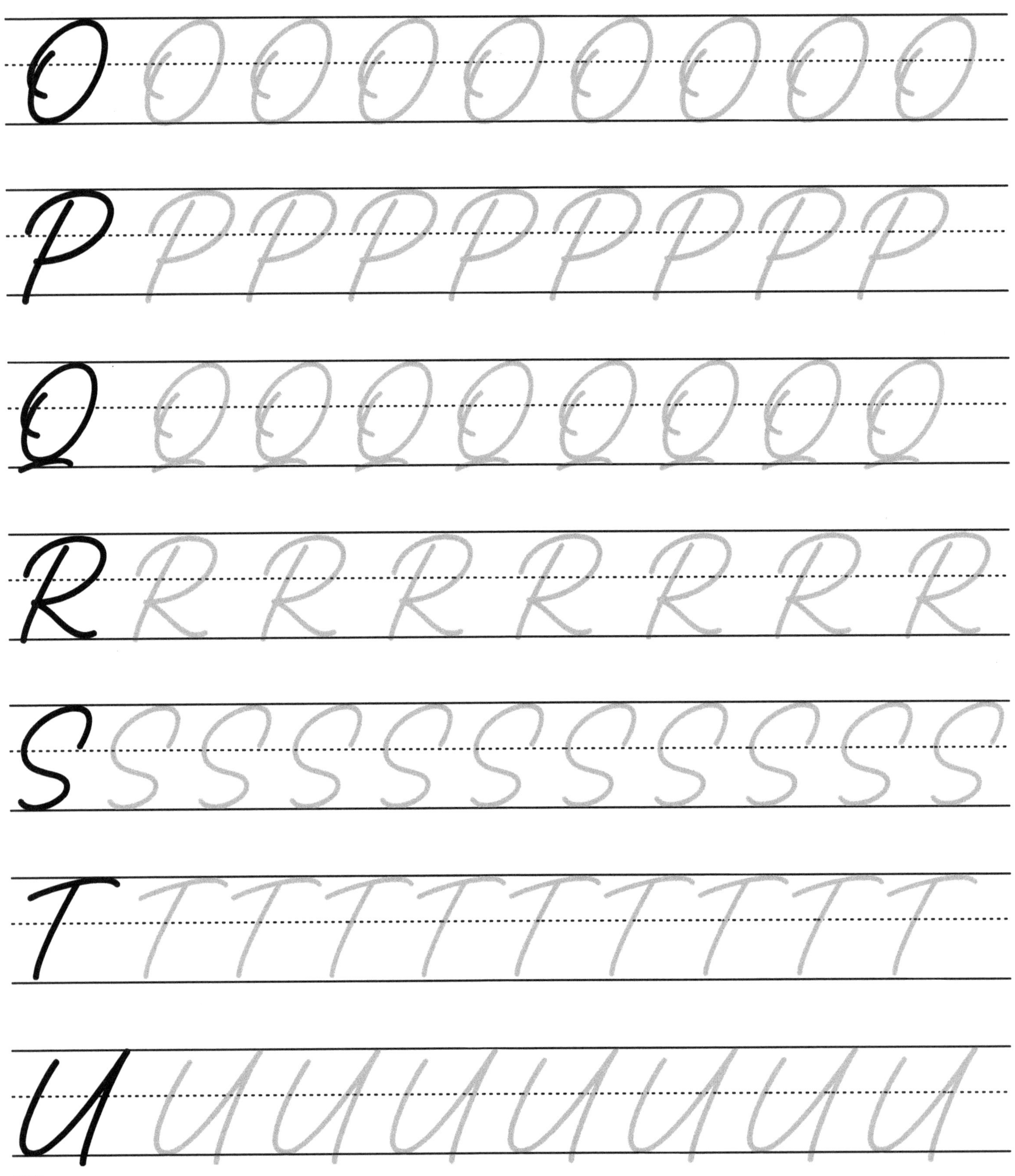

Practice Sheet

Basic Calligraphy

Practice Sheet

Basic Calligraphy

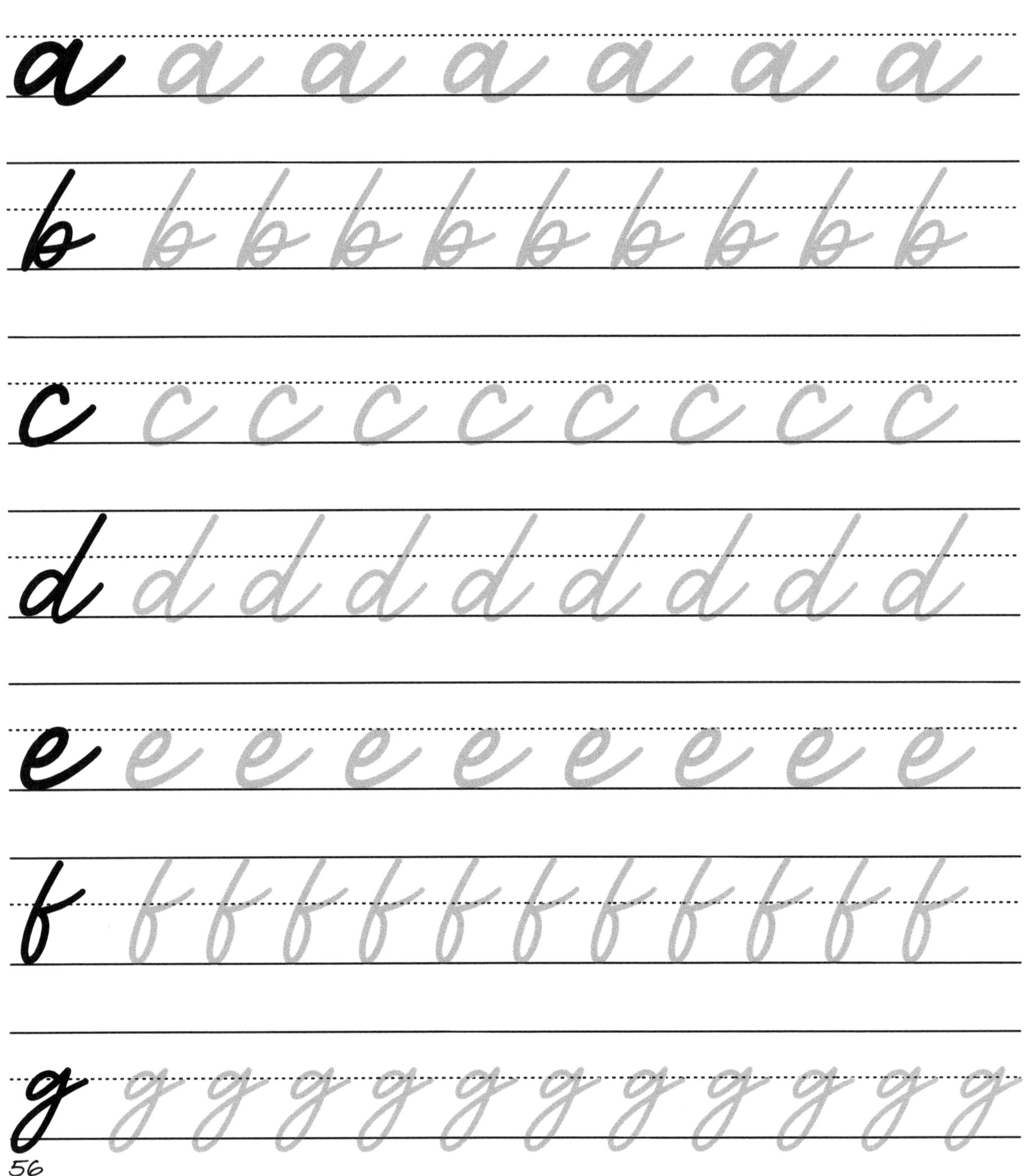

Practice Sheet

Basic Calligraphy

h h h h h h h h h

i i i i i i i i i i i i i

j j j j j j j j j j j j j j

k k k k k k k k k

e e e e e e e e e e e e e e e

m m m m m m m m m m

n n n n n n n n n n n

Practice Sheet

Basic Calligraphy

o o o o o o o o o o o o

p p p p p p p p p p p p

q q q q q q q q q q

r r r r r r r r r r r

s s s s s s s s s s s s

T T T T T T T T T T

u u u u u u u u u u u

Practice Sheet

Basic Calligraphy

Practice Sheet

Basic Calligraphy

0 0 0 0 0 0 0 0 0

1 1 1 1 1 1 1 1 1 1 1 1 1

2 2 2 2 2 2 2 2 2

3 3 3 3 3 3 3 3 3 3

4 4 4 4 4 4 4 4 4 4

5 5 5 5 5 5 5 5 5 5 5

6 6 6 6 6 6 6 6 6 6

Practice Sheet

Basic Calligraphy

NUMERIC DIGITS - CHARACTER ONE

7 7 7 7 7 7 7 7 7 7 7

8 8 8 8 8 8 8 8 8 8 8

9 9 9 9 9 9 9 9 9 9 9

10 10 10 10 10 10 10

21 21 21 21 21 21 21 21

32 32 32 32 32 32

43 43 43 43 43 43

Practice Sheet

Basic Calligraphy

Writing

Love

Beauty

Thank you

Sweet

Hello

Life

Practice Sheet

Basic Calligraphy

Sun

Moon

Sea

Wine

Family

Happiness

Freedom

Practice Sheet

Basic Calligraphy

Dreams

Passion

Art

Flowers

Time

Music

Heart

Practice Sheet

Angel *Angel Angel*

Stars *Stars Stars Stars*

Color *Color Color Color*

Perfume *Perfume*

Smile *Smile Smile*

Nature *Nature Nature*

Hope *Hope Hope Hope*

Practice Sheet

Basic Calligraphy

WORD COMPLETION EXERCISE - SECOND CHARACTER

Magic *Magic Magic*

Poetry *Poetry Poetry*

Pain *Pain Pain Pain*

Air *Air Air Air Air*

Adventure *Adventure*

Beach *Beach Beach*

Mountain *Mountain*

Practice Sheet

ヲヲ

ヲヲ

Basic Calligraphy

Dream

Hope

Laughter

Journey

Freedom

Butterfly

Flavor

Practice Sheet

Basic Calligraphy

Ink flows beautifully

Write with grace

Master every curve

Art through letters

Paper meets ink

Draw your words

Flourish your style

Practice Sheet

Basic Calligraphy

Letters come alive

Perfect every line

Ink your soul

Script with passion

Elegance in motion

Write your art

Feel every stroke

Practice Sheet

Basic Calligraphy

Flow with creativity

Ink shapes imagination

Lines build dreams

Letters hold stories

Capture every curve

Dance with ink

Shapes of beauty

Practice Sheet

Basic Calligraphy

Write your world

Embrace every letter

Lines create magic

Grace in script

Ink your vision

Words as art

Create timeless art

Practice Sheet

Basic Calligraphy

Dream big, work hard

Create. Inspire. Repeat

Ink your story.

Make it beautiful

Every stroke matters.

Words shape worlds

Art is timeless.

Practice Sheet

Basic Calligraphy

July 20, 1969

First Moon Landing

December 25, 2025

Christmas Day

April 15, 1912

Titanic Sinks

Practice Sheet

Basic Calligraphy

November 9, 1989

Fall of the Berlin Wall

July 4, 1776

Independence Day

October 31, 2023

Halloween Night

The end

Practice Sheet

Practice Sheet

"I would like to express my gratitude for purchasing this book. I would be immensely thankful if you could take a moment to share your feedback. This greatly helps the growth of our small business and allows us to reach more people.."